Strength

Strength

a play in three acts

by

Ely E. Pilchik

BLOCH PUBLISHING COMPANY
NEW YORK

Library of Congress Catalogue Card No.: 64–8822

PRINTED IN THE UNITED STATES OF AMERICA

DEDICATED

to all those wonderful Christians the world-over who helped my people in our blackest night.

The publication of this play was made possible thanks to the generosity of the family of the late

ABRAHAM H. PUDER
1889–1962

devoted husband, father, grandfather, brother and uncle.
A self-respecting Jew, a dedicated American, an effective community leader, a doer of stature.

"Who is strong? He who conquers the evil within him.

As it is said in the Book of Proverbs, 'Better is a patient man than a mighty one, and he who controls his temper than he who captures a city.'"

Rabbi Ben Zoma in Pirke Abot IV, 1

CHARACTERS

FRAU ERIKA TESHOW . . a widowed mother of about 40 in Act I
ANNA . . . . her older daughter of 18 in Act I
LISA . . . . her younger daughter of 16 in Act I
ERNST . . . . her son of 19 or 20 in Act I
THE FIRST DETECTIVE
THE SECOND DETECTIVE
THE MESSENGER FROM THE FOREIGN OFFICE
THE JAILER, Herr Flink
GUNTHER HEYDER . . . . . who becomes Lisa's husband.
JOHAN SCHTRICK . . . . . . who becomes Anna's husband.
LEGIONNAIRE PARETI
LEGIONNAIRE FAUBER
LEGIONNAIRE O'HARA
KURT RATHENAU
MIMI . . . . a Marseilles Fisherwoman
THE GENDARME
LEIBELE . . . . a refugee boy of about 14 or 15
SERELE . . . . his sister, aged 12
CHAYIM KADMI . . . . an underground Hagganah officer in his early twenties

Strength

Act I

ACT I

Time: The afternoon of June 26, 1922.

Scene: The living-room of a lower middle-class German home in Berlin. To the rear of the stage there are two windows heavily-curtained. Between the windows hangs a picture of a typical German father in a World War I uniform, draped in black indicating that he had been killed in that war. Stage right, a rocking chair with a handy side table. Frau Erika Teshow, about forty, greying slightly, wearing glasses, is reading a German newspaper. Stage left, a well-worn couch. In the room there are several additional chairs, a standing lamp, some flowers in a bowl. A clock of the Black Forest type is ticking away on the wall.

Frau Teshow (*Raising her head from the paper and looking to the door to her left*)
Anna—Anna my dear—

Anna (*off stage*)
Yes, Mamma

Frau Teshow Anna—a little coffee please, it must still be hot.

Anna (*off stage*)
Yes, Mother, one minute.
(*Frau Teshow returns to her paper. There is silence for half-a-moment. Anna enters with a demi-tasse in her hand. She is about 18, blond, very pretty if a little drawn. Smilingly she puts the demi-tasse on the side-table next to her mother's chair*)

Anna It was still hot, Mamma. Take a little sugar with it.

Frau Teshow No, no sugar, Anna, it spoils the lovely bitter taste of the coffee.
(*She raises the cup to her lips as Anna gently takes the newspaper from her and folds it*)

Anna Please, Mamma. Please, take the sugar. You need strength, sugar gives energy.

Frau Teshow (*Obviously pleased by her daughter's loving attentions*)
Me, Anna, strength, energy? You, my child, you need it, for the young men. Look how drawn your face is—it should be full.
(*She jokingly glances up and down her daughter's form and gestures*)
Yes, and that too should be full. Remember, Anna, young German men like plump, full, young German women.
(*She points to the picture*)

Yah, Pappa liked me those days, full, even fat—"*zafting,*" he used to say—"*zaftig ist gut.*"
(*She looks at the clock on the wall*)
Anna—it's past three o'clock already. Where is Lisa?

Anna Mamma, she will be back soon. She, well she told me she was going to the funeral after school.

Frau Teshow The funeral—why? What has she to do with the funeral? It's for Jews that funeral; he was a Jew.

Anna But Mamma, he was the Foreign Minister of the Republic. It's a state funeral, with all the officials, and the men in uniform. It's colorful and exciting for her.

Frau Teshow Exciting? What's exciting? A Jew is killed. Many have been killed in Germany before and many more will be killed in Germany during her lifetime.

Anna Mamma, please don't speak that way. He was a good Jew. He was a great German. He was one of the most important men in the war.

Frau Teshow Important? How important could he be? We lost the war—and Pappa was killed in the war.

(She weeps)

(From the door on the left, Lisa bursts in the door, all excited. She is about sixteen —flaxen blond hair, pink-cheeked, in a school uniform. She flings her books on the couch)

Lisa Mamma, Anna—You should have seen it. It was wonderful. Thousands, millions of people. I could hardly see the procession. I had to jump up and down to look over people's heads.

Frau Teshow Calm down, Lisa. Look how perspired you are. Go in, wash up—wash the sweat from your face. And what were you doing at the funeral anyway?

Lisa What was I doing? Mamma—Everybody was there. All of Berlin. And Gerda, and Mimi, and even Gunther.
(Lisa catches herself—Anna puts her finger to her lips)

Frau Teshow Gunther? Who's Gunther?

Lisa O, Nobody, Mamma, nobody.

Frau Teshow Gunther is nobody? How can somebody be nobody? How can nobody be Gunther?

Anna It's a young man, Mamma. A young man who once came around with Ernst.

Frau Teshow Yes, Ernst, shouldn't he be back? Did you see Ernst, at the funeral, Lisa?

Lisa No Mamma. How could I see my brother among the thousands in the streets? I saw only the backs of million heads. Well, some fronts. Mamma, you should have seen—it was so peculiar. A lot of people were crying, a lot were just laughing as though they were glad he was dead.

Frau Teshow Enough—no—enough Lisa. Take your books, and go. Go wash up. Your clothes are soaking with sweat.
(*Lisa grabs up her books—makes for the door on the right*)

Lisa Please, let me tell you about it. It's the most exciting thing I ever saw—
(*Her mother stares at her, Lisa gets the point*)
Well, later?
(*She leaves*)

Frau Teshow Anna, what was it Ernst said? A three day hike? Shouldn't he be back by now?

Anna Don't worry, Mamma. You know—young men, strong. He'll be in soon.

Frau Teshow That organization, Anna, what was it? Something about Germany rising again to full glory? What was it Anna?

(*She paces up and down—Anna becomes a little tense*)

Anna I don't really know, Mamma. Ernst is young and vigorous, and full of political ideas for himself and for Germany. He can't stand inferiority. He's a patriot, Mamma, like Pappa was. He's a son of the Fatherland.

Frau Teshow Yes, like Pappa. O Great God, let not happen to him what happened to Pappa.

Anna No, Mamma—the war is over. There will be no more wars. Ernst is very political. He listens to all the political speakers, to the grumblers and the shouters—it's natural Mamma.

Frau Teshow Yes, Anna, yes—but where is he? I'm getting nervous about it; Anna, I didn't sleep last night worrying about him. Where was the hike to? And who was the leader of the hike?

Anna Mamma, he wasn't very clear about it. You know Ernst, he doesn't tell everything. He broods and then he blurts. He's impulsive, Mamma.

Frau Teshow Impulsive, yes, impulsive—that's what worries me Anna.
(*There's a quiet rustle at the door to the*

left—the door opens slowly—Anna and Frau Teshow seem frozen, with their eyes fixed on the door. Ernst quietly enters—he is six feet, broad-shouldered, his blond hair mussed, his shirt torn, his pants messy)

Ernst Mamma, Anna—
(*He embraces first his mother, then his sister*)

Frau Teshow Ernst, my son, what is it? You're trembling—

Ernst Nothing, Mamma, has anyone been here looking for me—here?
(*The door to the right flings open—Lisa bursts in—her face is clean and fresh*)

Lisa Ernst, how was the hike? You should have seen the funeral—thousands, millions of
(*She runs toward him—upon hearing "Funeral," he turns pale—he pushes her away*)

Ernst Go Lisa, beat it, I want to talk to Mamma, and Anna. Beat it, Lisa—Go.

Lisa You big bloke—I wanted to tell you how exciting the funeral was—

Ernst (*Screaming*)
Go—Lisa—Get out of here!
(*Lisa cannot understand, she leaves*

through the right door. Frau Teshow and Anna are dazed. Ernst throws himself on the couch. They approach him to calm him)

Ernst Are you sure no one was here looking for me? Were you here all the time?

Frau Teshow No one—I was here all the time. Ernst, my son, what, what has happened? Tell us.

Ernst Nothing Mamma. Nothing—no one was here, hah?
(*Anna sits down, puts her arm around Ernst, smoothes his hair*)

Anna Tell us, Ernst, tell us. We're your family. We love you.

Ernst (*Bursting into tears*)
I did it. Herman and Friedrich and I did it—
(*He tears at his hair, twists and turns*)

Frau Teshow (*With a touch of hysteria*)
Did what my son? Did what? Who are Herman and Friedrich?
(*She stops in her tracks, points to the paper*)
Herman! Friedrich!
(*She screams*)
NO!

Anna Herman! Friedrich! The paper—No, Ernst, NO!

Ernst Yes, yes, I killed him. We killed him—maybe not I. They—they had the pistols, I had the hand-grenades—I threw—I killed.

Frau Teshow Oh, my son, my son—but, you're alive—you got away. They turned the pistols on themselves. They died on the spot.

Ernst Yes, they're lucky—they're gone.
(*He shouts*)
All of Germany is not looking for them, not hunting them down. They're looking for me, only for me.

Frau Teshow (*Regaining composure and strength*)
Anna, bolt the doors, the windows. Anna quick—
(*Anna stumblingly goes to the door left, then the first window, the second window, the door to the right*)
But why, Ernst, why?

Ernst Because he was a Jew-traitor. He was selling our Fatherland out to France, and to the Bolsheviks, the Russians.

Anna But Ernst, he was the Foreign Minister. He knew better than we. He was a great man in the war—head of supplies for our Armies.

Ernst Great man? A traitor. A Jew-dog. We lost the war.
(*He points to the picture and screams*)
Pappa was killed because that Jew betrayed us.

Anna Oh, no, Ernst—you've lost all—

Frau Teshow Never mind what he's lost—we must save him. We must hide him. Ernst, who were these Herman and Friedrich? I never saw them.

Ernst They were brave patriots, Mamma. They were of our Party to restore the glory of the Fatherland. We three were chosen to rid the nation of that Jew-traitor Rathenau. And we did. We did—it was his funeral that Lisa saw.

Frau Teshow Does anyone know you were the third, Ernst? Did anyone see?

Ernst I'm not sure Mamma, I'm not sure. But you can't trust anybody. The police—this weak democratic government which is destroying our Fatherland—has a million eyes.

Frau Teshow You must leave, Ernst. You must go to your uncle in Vienna, quickly. You must get out till everything quiets down.

Anna Come Ernst, Mamma's right. I'll help you pack. I'll take you to the railroad station.

Ernst No, no I can't leave now. I must report to the Party Leaders—there's more work to do. Rathenau was only the first—
(*A sharp rap on the door to the left*)

Frau Teshow (*whispering*)
Get him out of here—Schnell!
(*Anna takes Ernst by the hand—they leave quietly through the right door. The rap is repeated, more forcefully*)

Voice (*From outside*)
Teshow? Teshow?

Frau Teshow Yes
(*With iron composure*)
What is it?

Voice (*From outside*)
Open, please.

Frau Teshow One moment—
(*She goes to the door, unbolts it, opens—two men enter in street clothes*)

First Detective Teshow—Are you Frau Teshow?

Frau Teshow Yes, I am—

Second Detective We are from police headquarters—
(*they show their papers*)

Frau Teshow Indeed. And what can I do for you?

First Detective We are looking for a gentleman—

Frau Teshow My husband? I am sorry
(*She points to the picture*)
He is dead—killed in action at Verdun, defending the Fatherland.
(*Both detectives bow their heads*)

Second Detective Our deep sympathies.

Frau Teshow We are terribly sorry.

First Detective No, we are looking for a younger gentleman—about twenty. Some say his name was Ernst—tall, blond.

Frau Teshow Yes, yes, Ernst—my son—his name is Ernst. Yes, tall blond, true German,—but he's not here.

Second Detective Forgive us, Frau Teshow—it is our duty—we are only obeying orders. Where is your son?

Frau Teshow Ernst—he's on a hike, a three or four day hike. He left three days ago. Yes—what is today? Yes the 26th, is it? He left the morning of the 23rd—the 23rd, yes—with a group of twelve, perhaps more. On a hike—should be back tomorrow—tomorrow evening.

First Detective May we look around the house?
(*He starts toward the door on the right*)

Frau Teshow Look? Search my house? Why?
(*She points to the picture*)
Look behind that picture—that's where to look.
(*She trails the first Detective holding him back as he goes toward the door. The door bursts open—Ernst and Anna come out, Anna weeping bitterly*)

Ernst I am Ernst Teshow. You need look no further. What do you want of me?

First Detective Ernst Teshow, we arrest you for the murder of the Foreign Minister of the Republic, Walter Rathenau. Come with us to headquarters.

Frau Teshow No! He murdered no-one.
(*Dazed*)
On a hike—home—three days ago.
(*She gropes for her son. The First Detective takes hold of Ernst. The Second Detective gently holds Frau Teshow and tries to comfort her. Anna takes her from*

him—Ernst kisses his mother and sister as he's led away—)

Ernst *Auf Wiedersehen,* Mamma, Anna, for the glory of the Fatherland.
(*The three men leave—Anna and Frau Teshow are enwrapped in bitter tears*)

Frau Teshow His father's son, Anna. A patriot, a hero, Oh, how horrible—
(*Lisa dashes in—*)

Lisa What's the matter? Where's Ernst? What's happened?

Anna Sit down, Lisa—quiet. Let's help Mamma. Lisa, the police have taken Ernst away—

Lisa What did he do? Why?

Anna He did nothing, dear. They suspect him of having some connection with the Rathenau business.

Lisa The funeral—Ernst—is that why he—Ernst?
(*A rap at the door—Anna opens it—a man in uniform*)

Lisa More Police? They already took him. Go away.
(*She weeps*)

The Messenger I am from the Office of the Foreign Ministry—I have a letter for a Frau Erika Teshow—Is she here?
(*Anna points to her mother*)

The Messenger Ah yes, Frau Teshow? Sign this please.
(*Anna signs—she opens the letter—quietly she approaches her mother*)

Anna Mamma, it is a letter to you from the mother of Walter Rathenau, Frau Mathilde Rathenau—

END OF ACT I

Strength

Act II

Five years later

ACT II—SCENE I

Time: July 1, 1927, a little before noon.

Scene: A cell in a Berlin jail; stage right—the bars, with door. Stage center and left blacked out. Inside the cell a bed covered with a drab olive blanket. Books cover the floor of the cell and much of the bed. One light suspends from the ceiling, dim but possible to read by. Outside the cell—a chair near the door. Ernst is pacing up and down reading a sizable book and pronouncing with difficulty Hebrew words.

Ernst *Zedakah*—justice. *Chesed*—lovingkindness. *Zedakah*—justice. *Che . . .*
(*A Jailer, in uniform comes on from the dark mid-stage*)

The Jailer Teshow—Your last visitor—your mother. Last visitor on your first day of freedom.
(*Ernst puts the book down on the bed draws near the cell door. The Jailer goes out and quickly brings in Frau Teshow*)

Frau Teshow Ernst, my son, my son. This is the day.

The Jailer Only ten minutes. We have much paper work to do.

Ernst (*Kissing his mother through the bars and grasping her hands*)
Mamma, just a few more hours.
(*The Jailer leaves*)

Frau Teshow Yes, my son—yes, and we have a big dinner waiting at home, and Anna and Johan will be there with the children, and Lisa and Gunther—the whole family.

Ernst Mamma, how are they? Will Johan be promoted to principal of his school?

Frau Teshow Who knows? There is a Jewish teacher, who is his senior—

Ernst (*Painfully*)
Please, mamma—it will be all right. And Lisa and Gunther—are they very happy?

Frau Teshow She is the happiest girl in all Germany. Gunther is rising quickly in the Party. He is the Second or Third to Joseph Goebbels.

Ernst Goebbels?

Frau Teshow Yes, Ernst. You know, that lame genius. Hitler has named him the most important Nazi in Berlin. And he is brilliant. How he speaks? But you wouldn't know, would you?

Ernst No, I never saw or heard him. It's all been in these five years while I've been here.

Frau Teshow Yes, you will like Goebbels. And Gunther says, they need you very much in the Party—especially since you have been studying all that Jewish business, and Hebrew.

Ernst What do they need with that?

Frau Teshow Gunther says that the Party is establishing a special section on Jewish affairs. They will need you—all your studying here will get you a job in the Party right away.

Ernst (*Reflecting*)
Yes—Mamma, please return these books to the Berlin Library. Thank them for me. Here is the Hebrew Dictionary, and the Scriptures, Martin Buber's translation. Mamma, Buber's German is better than Martin Luther's.

Frau Teshow Ernst, how can you say that? How can a Jew translate the Holy Bible in good German?

Ernst (*Smiling*)
It is their Bible, Mamma. They know what it really means. Yes, and this "Introduction to the Talmud," thank the

Librarian. They were so good to me. *(She takes the books through the bars)*

Frau Teshow Yes, I will Ernst, and I will be waiting for you. Ernst?

Ernst Yes, Mamma.

Frau Teshow That letter—shall I take it with me?

Ernst No Mamma. I have it. I want to keep it with me always.

Frau Teshow Good—Ernst, my son, how I've been waiting for this day, to have you home again. My son at home.

The Jailer *(Enters and gestures)* Frau Teshow

Frau Teshow Yes, I'm going. The last kiss through these bars. My son—no more bars. *(She kisses him and exits with the Jailer. He returns and sits down)*

The Jailer Well Teshow—what can I do for you these last few hours?

Ernst Boxes, Herr Flink. Boxes to pack my books to take home.

The Jailer Yes—those books. So many books. You've made a university of this jail.

Ernst That's what I intended, Herr Flink. I took a five year course in this University. And, these are my professors—
(*pointing to the books*)
the greatest in the world. And you helped me, Herr Flink. You were the Chancellor of the University.
(*He laughs*)

The Jailer Flink the Jailer, Flink the failure, Chancellor of a University. You have a peculiar humor, Ernst.

Ernst It's not funny. It's true. You helped me get the books and the papers. You changed the bulb
(*pointing upward*)
when my light burned out. You were head of the university. Now I want to thank you. Wait—let me hold that till you give me my degree—the key to this cell-door.

The Jailer Don't thank me, Ernst. You're the professor. I learned a lot from you—talking with you, listening to you as you studied.

Ernst My education has just begun, Herr Flink. This is only five years. It takes fifty years really to learn something.

The Jailer The Chancellor of the University
(*jokingly pompous*)

wishes to state that the first year was wasted studying about a politician.

Ernst No, no, Herr Chancellor. Forgive me but you're wrong. Walter Rathenau, whose every written word I read here was not just a politician. He was one of the greatest Germans who ever lived. Remember this Herr Flink, Rathenau was a remarkable businessman; Rathenau was a deep thinker; Rathenau was a far-sighted statesman; all three in one.

The Jailer Bah, everybody says he failed.

Ernst No, Herr Flink. I failed. I failed to let him live so he could succeed in bringing order to Germany, order to Europe. I helped kill him just as he was beginning. (*He rebukes himself—banging at his cheeks and tearing at his hair*)

The Jailer Don't feel that way. It probably wasn't your hand-grenade. It was the bullets of those other two hoodlums. And anyway you have paid your penalty, you have served your time.

Ernst (*Reflectively*)
You know, Herr Flink, I think Rathenau might even have forgiven me. He had such a big heart.

The Jailer What was he? Some kind of preacher? Some kind of Rabbi?

Ernst No, Herr Flink, he was no preacher. He was a very practical businessman and a great statesman. But he did have a deep Jewish spirit. Do you know what he once said, Herr Flink? He said: 'When the Jew says he loves to hunt, he lies.'

(*A loud chorus of male voices is heard outside shouting:*
"Sieg Heil! Juda Verreke!
Sieg Heil! Deutschland Erwach!
Sieg Heil!"
[*And the strains of the Horst Wessel song:*]
Raise High the Flags!
Stand rank on rank together.
Storm Troopers march with steady, quiet tread—)

Ernst What—what is all that, Herr Flink?

The Jailer Oh, those hoodlums. The Brown Shirts. Hitler's bums. They're nobodies, they're nothings, forget them. You were saying about Rathenau—

(*The chorus sound drifts away*)

Ernst But they are so many, and they are so loud. What about this Hitler?

The Jailer He's a nobody. He's crazy. He's a bad painter from Vienna who never could make a living. So, he became a politician with a loud voice attacking Jews, and all the young bums, who refuse to work, gather around him and think of themselves as Officers and as very important. They think they are going to restore Germany to its real glory. Hoodlums—forget them.

Ernst I think my brother-in-law, Gunther, is caught up with them. Well, I was talking about Rathenau. He loved to quote our poet Heinrich Heine: 'There will come a time when freedom will speak everywhere and its language shall be Biblical.'

The Jailer Ah yes, the Bible.

Ernst The Bible, Herr Flink. Rathenau was brought up on the Bible. In its real language—not translation. So after reading everything Rathenau had written, I began studying the language of his Bible, Hebrew. That was my second and third year course in this University, Herr Chancellor. And I've learned much of it. I can read the Old Bible. Not all, the Prophets and Job are very hard, but lots of it I can read in the Hebrew.

The Jailer Hebrew—it must be difficult, like Arabic.

Ernst Yes, Hebrew is related to Arabic. They are sister-languages of one Semitic mother. How do you happen to mention Arabic, Herr Flink?

The Jailer Oh, I knew a little once—couldn't read it —could speak a little.

Ernst Did you learn it at school?

The Jailer (*Laughing*)
Yah, some school—some university. The Sahara Desert University.

Ernst You were in the Sahara? Why?

The Jailer Oh, I tried the French Foreign Legion for a while. Ran away from some trouble I got into in Hamburg, my native town.

Ernst How was life in the Foreign Legion? In the Sahara?

The Jailer That's not life. That's a living death. The sun burning the sand all day. The cold at night. Murderous Arabs always waiting in ambush—
(*A voice from off-stage: "Flink, unlock the door. Release the prisoner Teshow. Bring him to the Office"*)

The Jailer *Jah Wohl.*
(*Flink takes his key, opens the door*)

Your diploma, Ernst.

(Ernst walks out, one book under his arm —he looks back—the two men walk off stage rear)

END OF SCENE I of ACT II

ACT II—SCENE II

Time: Three hours later.

Place: The Teshow living room, same as in Act I; but a large table covered with food, bottles of white wine, Bock beer, etc. is in the center of the room. Around the table are Frau Teshow, Anna and her husband Johan, Lisa and her husband Gunther, and Ernst. The women wear light cotton dresses in gay colors. The men, plain pants open white shirts except for Gunther who wears the official uniform of the Brownshirts, Swastika and all. Much laughter and gaiety as the curtain rises.

Gunther (*Getting up, with bottle in hand, going toward Ernst*)
A little more wine, more *Riesling* Ernst —this is a banquet for a hero—drink up.

Ernst (*Waving him gently away*)
No, thank you. Enough, my insides aren't used to such good food and drink.

Lisa To our hero. To Ernst. Another toast.
(*They all raise their glasses, some wine, some beer and they drink. Ernst does not look pleased*)

Gunther To another Hero. To Horst Wessel:
(*They burst into song—Gunther, Johan, and Lisa with great enthusiasm—Anna and Frau Teshow moderately*)
"Raise High the Flags! Stand Rank on Rank Together
Storm Troopers march with steady, quiet tread—"

Johan Many do regard you as a hero, Ernst. They say that you, and the others, began this new Party. They speak about the shots that launched the new Germany.

Gunther Yes, Ernst. Now they are waiting for you. Come tonight Ernst—My leader, Dr. Joseph Goebbels wants to meet you.

Lisa Oh, he's quite a man.

Ernst What do you mean, Lisa?

Lisa Well, last week when he was at our flat talking secret politics with Gunther, he looked more at me than he did at Gunther. Didn't he, my love?
(*She looks proudly at her young husband*)
And he patted me right over here.
(*She pats her thigh.*)

Gunther Don't be so proud, my dove. Dr. Goebbels has an eye and a hand for all the beautiful German girls.

Anna It's disgusting—

Frau Teshow Come children. Behave. I'd better get a pot of fresh coffee.
(*She exits left*)

Ernst What would this Herr Goebbels want with me?

Gunther You're one of the few men the Party can trust who knows about Jews. Haven't you been studying about those swine since you've been in jail?

Ernst (*Wincing, yet controlling his temper*)
I've been studying about people, Jewish people; they are the farthest thing from swine. They are forbidden the flesh of swine in their Torah.

Johan Gunther gets excited, Ernst. He is so enthusiastic. Easy now Gunther. Let me explain. You see Ernst, the Nazi Party is very interested in the Jews. They need experts on the Jewish problem. And you are an expert because you've read so much about them. Aren't you?

Ernst I'm hardly an expert. I've read their history and some of their philosophy. I've studied their language and their Scriptures.

Johan Exactly. You are more expert than most of the leaders in the Party.

Gunther Not more than Dr. Goebbels.

Johan Well, Goebbels knows some. But he is mostly a great voice. He needs a man of background behind him.

Gunther Goebbels is a genius. He taught the youth to understand about the Jews.

Ernst Strange, I never heard of him.

Anna How could you fail to hear him. He does nothing but shout all over Germany.

Johan Hush Anna.
(*He shows his dominating impatience, Anna recoils*)
This is conversation for men. Get me another beer.
(*She leaves stage left*)
You say you have read Goebbels' speeches, Ernst?

Gunther What have you been reading about Jews then all these years?

Johan Easy Gunther. I'm surprised, Ernst. Let me just give you a few of his points. He says that there are only two pure races in the world, the Aryans and the Jews. The

Aryans are masters—they must guard the purity of their race.

Ernst Why that's nonsense. Jesus, the Saviour, was a Jew.

Johan No, no dear Ernst.
(*His anger rises a little*)
That's not nonsense. I'm a teacher. One day soon, I'll be a professor. I say to you that is fact. This is true philosophy. And furthermore, Jesus was not a Jew. Goebbels makes that clear. He says: "Whoever claimed that Jesus was a Jew was either being stupid or telling a lie."
(*He raises his voice more*)
Jesus was an Aryan, like we Germans.
(*Anna returns with two bottles of beer, she pours one in Johan's mug*)

Gunther That's what Julius Streicher says all the time in his great paper "*Der Stuermer.*" And who cares about Jesus anyway. He was a weakling. We must purge the German mind of Jesus as we must purge the German land of Jews.

Anna Gunther, that is heresy—

Johan (*Interrupting his drink and rising, pointing at Anna*)
Anna stay out of this. Women belong in

the kitchen and in the other place. Not in serious discussions among men.

Ernst I just don't understand, I can't believe my ears. Must be too much wine. I cannot follow you.

Gunther What's happened to that man? Isn't he the man who killed Rathenau and opened the way to our Party and our glory. What have they done to you in jail?

Ernst They were very kind to me. They permitted me to think and to read. They provided me with books. The Berlin Library was very gracious. Yes, they permitted me to think things through for myself. I was one of those who took part in the assassination of Rathenau, and then I began getting acquainted with the man I killed. I read what he believed. He was a great German—a great man.

Gunther An enemy of Germany. A traitor, like all the Jews.

Ernst No, no, no Gunther. He loved Germany. He sought the best for Germany. He helped develop the great electrical plant of Germany. He tried to restore Germany after the war. Have you read Rathenau, Gunther?

Gunther I read Hitler. I read the inspired words of the Fuehrer. I must tell Goebbels to have all of Rathenau's books in Germany burned.

Ernst Burn books?

Johan Yes, Ernst. Some books must be burned if they confuse and distort the minds of citizens. I am a teacher, a professor. I know what books can do to children's minds.

Ernst (*Getting a little angry*)
Before you burn Rathenau's books let me tell you what he believed.

Gunther Who cares—

Lisa Let him talk Gunther. He's older than you.
(*Gunther threatens to strike Lisa. Johan and Anna grab his hand*)

Johan Very well, Ernst—
(*mockingly*)
What did Rathenau have to say?

Ernst There are five volumes of Rathenau's works, written in a beautiful German style. But his thought in a word was this: He believed in development, human development. He said that man has gone through three stages: first, pre-historic man who was driven only by instinct; second, historic man who is guided by intellect and purpose; and the third stage is that of man of the future, when he will fulfill himself in the kingdom of the soul.

Gunther Never mind that business of man's soul. That's weak Christianity. There is only a national soul. The national soul of Germany—Germany over everything.

Johan That's interesting Ernst—but let's wait with the future. Let's deal with the present. Now how was that historic man? That's it, driven by intellect and purpose. The Nazi party is concerned with historic man. It draws from the greatest intellects. Nietschze who taught us about the coming of superman—Chamberlain who calls us the super-race—and Hitler himself who gives us purpose as a great nation.

Gunther And Putzi—

Ernst Putzi? Who is Putzi?

Johan Putzi Hanfstaengl, a graduate of Harvard University—a great friend of Hitler. Brilliant.

Lisa Yes, and Hitler is in love with his sister.

Gunther (*Angry*)
Lisa!
(*She freezes*)

Ernst Somehow, I haven't read these great intellects. I guess I've been wasting my time with Kant and Goethe and Schiller.

Anna Please, please let's stop this political talk, and let's just be a family. This is a happy hour.

Johan Anna, I warn you again—

Gunther Politics is everything. We're on the march. Our Party will conquer the world. But first we must butcher out the Jews and the Communists.

Ernst Butcher out the Jews?
(*In anger he goes at Gunther. Gunther, fists up, goes at Ernst. Frau Teshow enters with pot of coffee*)

Frau Teshow Here, fresh wonderful coffee.
(*She recognizes the situation*)
Stop! Gunther, Ernst—Stop! Like little children.
(*Johan, Anna, and Lisa pull Ernst and Gunther apart*)
What is it? You are brothers. Ernst, Gunther. What in all the world can so anger you?

Gunther Ernst has been talking traitorous things here. Like an enemy of Germany.

Ernst It's nothing, Mamma. Here, give me some of your good fresh coffee.
(*She pours him a cup*)

Frau Teshow But what can it be?

Johan Ernst has filled his mind with a lot of Jewish propaganda, and he takes it seriously. He has no understanding of our times, of our thought, of our leaders.

Frau Teshow So give him some time. He will get his bearings. He will read the papers. He will meet people. He has just come back home.

Ernst No, no, Mamma. It's more serious than that. True, I am not up to date. I thought I was; they did give me the daily papers.

Gunther Did they give you "Der Stuermer"—Streicher's—

Ernst Is that a newspaper?

Gunther (*Angry again*)
It's the only newspaper worth reading in Germany.

Ernst You see Mamma, I feel such a deep intolerance in this room. There is a wild kind of spirit. Like that of beasts. I hear such words as, "Butcher the Jews."

Gunther It's the only way.

Frau Teshow Please, boys, please. Let's have peace here in our home.

Gunther There can be no peace with enemies of Germany.

Anna Johan—we must go. Remember the children were not feeling well.

Johan Yes Anna. Get some rest Ernst. We will talk, I will explain, I will teach you.
(*They prepare to leave*)

Lisa Come Gunther. I must prepare for Dr. Goebbels tonight. I haven't a thing in the house.

Gunther I'm coming Lisa. Yes we must have a little feast tonight for the great Goebbels—
(*He looks at Ernst*)
Perhaps Mamma, you're right. Some rest, meeting a few people, and Ernst will come back to himself. You hear Ernst? To me and to my Party you are a hero. We welcome you back. Come and March with us. *Sieg Heil!* If you shake off this foolishness you talked about, come to the flat tonight —at nine. Dr. Goebbels and I will be

there waiting for you. Thank you, Mamma, for the feast.

Lisa (*Kisses her mother, approaches Ernst. He kisses Her*)
Thank you, Mamma, what wonderful food. *Auf Wiedersehen,* Anna and Johan—
(*Gunther and Lisa wave—and they depart stage left*)

Johan See Ernst, how good of Gunther to understand your confusion. And to forgive you. And to invite you to meet Goebbels. What a privilege, Ernst. Don't pass it up.

Anna Johan may be right, Ernst. It's a start. You could begin work immediately.
(*Frau Teshow nods her head approvingly*)

Ernst Doing what?

Johan Let me explain again, Ernst. Goebbels is very close to Hitler. He poses as an expert on the Jewish problem. But he needs help. He needs a man like you who knows Hebrew and Jewish history and can deal with the Jews—in these early stages. You could enrich the Party, Ernst. You know the passages in the Jewish Writings where the Jews condemn all those who are not Jews. This is exactly the propaganda we need to inflame the minds of the Germans

Frau Teshow (*Goes over to Ernst, lovingly strokes his head*)
Sit down, my son. Here take some fresh coffee.

Ernst (*Sitting down, sipping*)
Mamma, I am bewildered—I never dreamt —I never believed—

Frau Teshow (*Taking some coffee*)
Ah, my son. The world doesn't stand still. As your father used to say—
(*She points to the picture*)
Things move fast. They have rushed these bad five years. There is trouble in Germany, Ernst. We have never recovered from the defeat in the war. Our government is weak. Our spirits are broken. Our pride as a nation is shattered. We are a great people, Ernst—but we are down. The other nations have their boots on our necks. They won't let us come back to our greatness.

Ernst They are trying, Mamma. They stopped demanding reparations. We can join the family of nations as a democracy.

Frau Teshow You must be realistic my son. There is unemployment. The young men, like yourself, are restless. They want position like Gunther. They want promotion like

Johan. And now they've found a leader. A great German Fuehrer is calling them —this man Hitler is a God-send.

Ernst But, Mamma—I hear he's a nothing. A paperhanger or some cheap painter. An agitator in beer-halls. He's gathered around him hooligans.

Frau Teshow Oh, my son—you've been reading Communist propaganda. The Jewish press. His enemies seek to defame him.

Ernst No, Mamma. Herr Flink, the Jailer, told me. And he knows. He has been around this world—Africa and France.

Frau Teshow The Jailer? Think Ernst, think. What would he say? His livelihood depends upon the government in power. The government that Hitler challenges. He was feeding you political propaganda, trying to save his own skin.

Ernst I can't believe that Mamma. He's not an educated man, but he is intelligent and experienced and he was a good friend.

Frau Teshow You are so naive, my son. People sell their souls for a crust of bread. People's tongues are their picks and shovels, their tools for getting or holding on to jobs.

Ernst Not all people, Mamma. There are honest people, many. The soul is not a tool, Mamma. Walter Rathenau said: "The soul is not a weapon."

Frau Teshow Forget Rathenau, my son. That's the bitter past. Open your mind to the future, to the living, the rising. You have such an opportunity. As the boys said, with Dr. Joseph Goebbels. You would rise to the top quickly in the Party.

Ernst By lying about Jews? By condemning people? By, as they said, butchering?

Frau Teshow Gunther is so young, and so zealous. You mustn't take him all that seriously. All this Jew business is only a means, a good technique for the Party to come to power.

Ernst It's so brutal, Mamma. So un-Christian. We are a Christian family—you taught us from the New Testament. When I was a baby you would read me the Sermon on the Mount. Five years ago I forgot it. I lost my head. But I forgot it once, only once. I came back to it in my jail cell when I read the Hebrew prophets. "Do justly, love mercy, walk humbly." This is the true and only way Mamma. I want to live right—I want to repent the evil I did.

Frau Teshow My son, my son, listen to me. This is not a religious world. We live each day in practical circumstances. The daily bread, the daily roof over our heads, the daily facts of life. I don't know—maybe the teachings of the Church distract us from these hard facts. Maybe we will someday come back to the religious way. But now Ernst, we must see things as they are. You are a young man. I want you to have a great future. Hitler is the man of the future. Attach yourself to him and rise, my son, rise.

Ernst Mamma, I don't understand you. I thought it was only my brothers-in-law. But you—Mamma—how can you be taken in by this rubbish—this Nazi filth. Because 50 or 70,000 have gone crazy with a wild illusion of power, of German glory, you have lost all your balance.

Frau Teshow (*Upset*)
Balance, Ernst? I have my balance. I want happiness for my children. A future—for you and for Anna and for Lisa and for my grand-children. Your father died for that. For the glory of the Fatherland. Now we have a chance. We have a leader. I cannot let old, sentimental weak ideas stand in their way. Take hold of yourself, Ernst. Get in there with the Party and rise with it to victory and prosperity.

Ernst Mamma, over innocent people's heads?

Frau Teshow There are no innocent and there are no guilty, Ernst. There are only the strong and the weak. The superior and the inferior. You are strong, Ernst.

Ernst (*Aroused*)
Perhaps, perhaps, stronger than you think, Mamma.

Frau Teshow Forget all that dreamy reading, Ernst. This is a time for action. Go, Go tonight, meet Dr. Goebbels. Begin to work. Play your role as a German hero.

Ernst Mamma—calm down a little. Let me remind you of the letter. Let me recall to you the spirit of the letter.

Frau Teshow A scrap of paper, Ernst. Tear it up. Forget it. Forget papers and books. We are not a nation of lazy writers and thinkers, Ernst. We are a nation of soldiers. Go join the legion marching to victory, Ernst.

Ernst What did you say Mamma?

Frau Teshow (*With strong voice*)
I said, go join the legion marching to victory. For the victory of the future. Join Hitler's legion. Up front, Ernst, up front.

Ernst (*With reflection*)
Yes, Mamma, I shall do just that. This is

not the home I thought I came from. These are not my sisters and my brothers, this is not the nation I thought it was. This is not my spirit. This is not my country. I am a man without a home, without a family, without a country. Now I know. My head is clear. Mamma, you showed me the way. I shall go and join the legion—(*He rises, a glow comes over his face, and he shouts*) Vive la France!

END OF ACT II

Strength

Act III

Fifteen years later

ACT III

Time: The Spring of 1942, early evening

Scene: A French Foreign Legion Outpost in the Algerian Sahara. Half the stage is used —the right half; the left half is blacked out. The floor is sand, rather thick. A sizable tent flying the French flag is set up. It is closed—a light barely visible in it. Just outside, on guard, Legionnaire Pareti sits squatted playing the *Marseillaise* on his harmonica. A moment after curtain rises Legionnaire Fauber enters from the dark off stage center.

Fauber What's all the patriotism, Pareti?
(*Pareti rises—he is very cheerful*)

Pareti Sure patriotism—Vive la France—What a performance, what a performance.
(*He points toward the entrance to the tent*)

Fauber Oh, the Adjutant—*oui,* one for the books —how many did he nab?

Pareti Twenty-four, twenty-four supermen. Aryan supermen. He caught 'em with their guns and pants on—the Fox's finest.

Fauber I heard, I heard, formidable (French pronunciation), *magnifique.* Just how did he do it?

Pareti I don't know the exact details—you know, he doesn't talk—not even about this strange man. Like nothing happened—just another day's routine.

Fauber Well how? How? What's the word?

Pareti I got it from O'Hara—he was on guard nearby. It was like this: General Rommel was rolling ahead with a big mob from his *Afrika Korps* and left behind these 24 brilliant krauts to watch the rear. Up comes our Adjutant, out of the blue, with a sawed-off sub-machine gun—all by himself, disguised in a Nazi Officer's uniform and shouts at them "*Achtung, Achtung*" in perfect German accent.

Fauber Yes, he sure knows his German language—and every other language I guess.

Pareti Well, they stopped dead, like Sphynxes in the sand. He ordered them to throw their weapons to the ground, called for O'Hara, and the 24 of them goose-stepped right on into the Foreign Legion Headquarters—the Adjutant and O'Hara at their backs.

Fauber And that was all there was to it?

Pareti That does it. One Legionnaire captures 24 of Rommel's geniuses. Now how can they win this war?

Fauber Oh, don't underestimate that General Rommel, he's sweeping across all North Africa.

Pareti We'll get him. We'll get them all. C'mon let's celebrate.
(*He goes back to the harmonica playing the* Marseillaise *while Fauber joins in singing. After a few moments Legionnaire O'Hara enters from darkened stage back with a new man*)

Fauber O'Hara—hallo—Who's your friend?

Pareti Yeh, is that the 25th you're bringing in.

O'Hara Now—just a new recruit sent from Headquarters to our unit.
(*He turns to the new man*)
Wait here, a moment.
(*He enters the tent*)

Pareti Where you from?

Rathenau Originally?

Fauber Yes, originally. I'm from Cannes, the Riviera—just regular French. Pareti here's from Naples, we have lots of Italians now in the Legion. Where are you from?

Rathenau From all over, I guess. I've been to Cannes. I've been to Naples. Where haven't I been? Originally from Berlin.

Pareti Berlin? You're German?

Rathenau Oh, they wouldn't think so back there. My family has only lived in Germany for 500 years—but I'm not Aryan—I'm a Jew. (*O'Hara comes out of the tent and points Rathenau in*)

Fauber He's a Jew from Germany originally. Nice, soft-spoken—like an aristocrat. (*The Adjutant comes out of the tent, folds over a part of the canvas giving a full view of the interior. An electric light hangs from above like unto the one in the jail cell in Act II. There is a desk, a bed, and dozens, upon dozens of books. The Adjutant is about 40 with a heavy mustache*)

The Adjutant Pareti, O'Hara, Fauber—dismissed until I call.
(*The three salute and go off stage center to the rear*)

The Adjutant (*Back behind his desk to Rathenau standing before him*)
Now tell me your name again.

Rathenau Kurt Rathenau, *mon Adjutant Chef.*

The Adjutant And your home?

Rathenau Berlin, Germany.

The Adjutant Do you happen to be a Jew?

Rathenau I am.

The Adjutant I like your people. I know something about them. A great people. I've read your Bible in the original Hebrew, even a little Talmud. And some Maimonides —Oh, Maimonides.

Rathenau (*Amazed*)
You know more about our literature than I do.

The Adjutant (*Laughs*)
Only a little—just a little. Tell me Rathenau, do you by any chance happen to be related to the man who was the Foreign Minister of Germany some years ago, Walter Rathenau?

Rathenau He was my uncle, mon Adjutant Chef.

The Adjutant (*Jumps up from his seat*)
You say your uncle?

Rathenau My uncle sir, my father's brother. He was murdered by those who later murdered all Germany.

The Adjutant Yes, I know. But that's not quite right. Hold on, Rathenau and listen to me. My name is not Tessier, I am not French. I am German. My real name is Ernst Teshow. I was one of the three men who murdered your uncle on the morning of June 24, 1922. The other two turned the pistols on themselves and committed suicide on the spot. I escaped, but not for long—the police arrested me in my home two days later. Sit down Rathenau, this is a long story, I've waited fifteen years to tell it.
(*Rathenau sits down on the bed just dazed*)
Here's a cigarette—
(*He lights it for him*)
A little cognac—
(*He pours him a glass*)
Now listen to me as I pour out my soul—Rathenau.

Rathenau *Jah, mon Adjutant Chef.*

Ernst They gave me a long prison term because they found that the pistol-bullets got him, my hand-grenade missed. They spared my life. Then they shortened my prison term—they released me after five years. And, in those five years I began repenting. I first began reading your uncle's writings—here, I have all five volumes of his work. (*He picks up a book and hands it to Rathenau*)

Rathenau "*Demokratische Entwicklung*," The Development of Democracy."

Ernst Yes, that's some fine democracy the Nazis developed. Well, I began to study the Jewish Bible—your uncle's Bible—and the language of that Bible. I learned your prophets by heart—"*Nachamu, nachamu ami*—" "Comfort, comfort, my people," declared your prophet Isaiah and I decided to devote the rest of my life to bringing comfort to the people of Walter Rathenau. To try to cleanse myself of my guilt. And I've done a little—
(*He points to stage left as the desert scene blacks out. The other side of the stage lights up on the fish market in Marseille—by the docks. Mimi, about 50, dressed mussily in typical fisherwoman attire presides over an outdoor counter loaded with fish. A scale hangs nearby. A couple of boxes are scattered around. Another fish counter is seen*)

Mimi Fresh caught fish—fresh caught fish (*in a chant*) fresh caught fish.

(*A French Gendarme slowly goes by, he smells the fish*)

Gendarme The fish smell fresh—but the scale, Mimi have you fixed it? Is it a little more honest than it was yesterday?

Mimi (*With contempt*)
Honest, as honest as those Nazis whose boots you lick.

Gendarme Mimi, careful. I'll report you.

Mimi Report, report. You have a lot of power over little people like me, but nothing over those beasts, the invaders. Go lick their boots—bow and scrape to them.

Gendarme Hold your tongue, Mimi, what can I do? I obey orders. I must make a living. The Maginot Line couldn't hold them. You want me to stand up to the whole German Army?
(*A Nazi Officer enters from stage rear—as he draws closer Ernst's face is visible*)
(*The Gendarme salutes him*)

Ernst What goes on here conspiracy against the Reich? You Frenchmen can't be trusted for a moment. I'll arrest both of you in a minute.
(*He gestures firmly to the Gendarme*)

Heraus! Tout de Suite!
(*The Gendarme bows, salutes, and leaves.*)

Mimi Ernst—a letter.
(*She takes out a letter*)

Ernst Finally, thank God. (*He quickly opens it*) From Mamma—she's fine.

Mimi And the family, what's new?

Ernst *Ach,* some good, some bad—Mamma's alright, she's still working at the hospital, day and night she says. Many wounded. Yes, and Johan got that professor position at the University. Anna is happy—always asking about me. Her children—the boy getting ready to go in the Army, the girl in the Hitler Youth Gang. And Lisa, poor Lisa.

Mimi What—what happened to her?

Ernst It would be funny if it were not so tragic—it's a peculiar poetic justice. Her husband, Gunther, high up in the party, preferred to ride his motorcycle into Paris instead of the limousine, for Hitler's grand entrance. On the highway, just before coming into the city, his motorcycle stalled, and one of the fast-moving Panzer tanks ran over him and crushed him. It stopped the whole procession. Hitler ordered that the tank-driver be shot on the spot. What an end to a Nazi zealot. He never lived to see the promised city. Poor Lisa, *Ach,* this madness.

Mimi It's hard for me to cry for him.

Ernst Don't try—I can't either.
(*He draws near her and whispers*)
Mimi, the children.

Mimi (*Quietly*)
They're right in the house—shall I get them?

Ernst Yes, in one minute.
(*He shouts*)
Gendarme!
(*The Gendarme comes running*)

Gendarme (*Saluting*)
Yes Sir.

Ernst Get a partner and shut off this street. You hear me? You cover that side, he covers the other. Nobody gets through. Did you hear me?

Gendarme Yes Sir!

Ernst Quick! (*to Mimi*) Now, bring them out.
(*Mimi leaves, Ernst re-opens the letter—*

reads it again, sighs. Mimi returns with Leibele and Serele. They are shabbily dressed and terribly frightened as they see the Nazi uniform)

Mimi Don't be afraid children, he is a friend. His uniform is a disguise.

Serele (*Whispering*)
I don't believe it. Don't trust them, Leibele.
(*She holds tight to her brother*)

Mimi Children, this is Ernst—he will get you to the ship. Ernst, this is Leibele Perelman and his sister, Serele.

Ernst *Shalom,* Leibele. *Shalom,* Serele, *U'vracha.*
(*He extends his hand to them. Serele clings tighter to Leibele. The boy, after some hesitation, cooly extends his hand*)

Leibele *Shalom.*

Ernst Come children, sit down, let's get acquainted.
(*Leibele sits on a box—Serele hangs on to him. Ernst sits down on another box. Mimi keeps a watch-out, standing behind her fish counter*)

Mimi Fresh-caught fish! Fresh-caught fish!

Ernst Here Serele, here Leibele—oranges from Jaffa, Jaffa oranges from the Golden land of Israel.

(*The children's eyes pop out. Leibele takes an orange—Serele hesitates*)

Serele (*To her brother*)

Poisoned, Leibele?

Leibele (*Unpeeling the orange, eating a segment, giving her a segment*)

No, no poison, Serele. Oh, it's so wonderful—it's been so long.

(*They gobble up the orange, Serele finally extends her hand and takes the other orange from Ernst. She starts peeling it, giving Leibele segments of it as she eats*)

Serele Good, sweet.

(*She begins to unfreeze—detaches herself a little from Leibele, then sits down between the two men on the boxes, retaining a grip on Leibele's leg*)

Ernst Now, that's better. You're going to the land where these oranges grow. And from now on it will always be good and sweet. Soon the captain of the ship will come to take you—it's just off the dock here. Don't be afraid. He too will be wearing a uniform like this. But, he's of your people—a Hagganah officer disguised as a Nazi.

Leibele You hear Serele—Hagganah.
(*He bursts into smiles*)

Serele Hagganah.
(*She forces a smile, still quite unsure*)

Mimi Fresh-caught fish, fresh-caught fish.

Ernst Now Leibele—would you tell me what happened to you, or is it too painful. I am not just curious. But what you tell me might help us get other children out.

Leibele Sure, I'll talk. We left a lot of children back there. Frightened, hungry children. What they would give for an orange.

Ernst I have just one more here. Will you divide it equally?

Leibele Serele can have it all.

Serele No, you Leibele, you have it all. You were so thirsty most of the time.

Ernst Well, let's settle it—let's just settle this great big quarrel.
(*He peels the orange—splits it in half and gives to each*)
That was easy.

Serele Good. Oh, it is so good.

Ernst Where was your home?

Leibele Baranovitch, Poland. We had a big brick house on *Ulitza Senatorska,* facing the main market square.

Serele And a big back-yard with two swings and a see-saw and little chicks and ducklings.

Mimi Fresh fish, fresh-caught fish.
(*The sound of siren screeching is heard. Serele, panicky, jumps up and wraps her arms about Leibele*)

Ernst Sh—sh! There is nothing to be afraid of.

Serele Gestapo! Gestapo.
(*She cries*)

Ernst No Gestapo, Serele. It's a military police car. No one can harm you while I'm here. No one can ever harm you any more. All that is over. You're going to the land of Israel. Don't be afraid Serele.
(*She relaxes a little. Slowly sits down again, but clutches Leibele's leg*)
Now, back to *Baranovitch* and *Ulitza* what?

Serele (*Quietly*)
Senatorska, by the market.

Ernst Ah, yes *Senatorska.* Now tell me, your father, your mother?
(*Serele begins to weep—draws closer to Leibele*)

Leibele Sha, Serele—if we tell about it more and more it will be easier. My father was a Doctor—a good Doctor.

Serele And he used to call me his little nurse—because I used to help him. I'd make the children say 'Ah—ah' when he looked in their throat.

Ernst (*Wiping a tear from his eye*)
And you will be a big nurse when you come to the land of Israel, and maybe you will help another Doctor, who will be your husband, Serele.

Leibele My father was the Doctor to Jewish people and many Christian people also came to him.

Serele Even nuns and priests and Polish officers.

Ernst He must have been a very good Doctor.

Serele The best Doctor in all *Baranovitch.* The best Doctor in the whole *Minsker Gubernye.*

Ernst I'm sure, I'm sure of that.

Leibele Then the Nazis came to *Baranovitch.* We will never forget the date, the 27th of June, 1941—it was a Friday morning.

Serele Early in the morning, they woke me up. I peeked out of the window, they covered the whole market square with motorcycles and trucks, and tanks—Swastikas all over.

Leibele Everyone was terribly frightened. We started hiding away the food we had. My mother was so scared—but my father was brave. He kept telling her, "They will not harm us."

Mimi Fresh fish, fresh-caught fish.

Leibele 'I am a Doctor,' he kept telling her, 'They will need me, even enemies need Doctors.'

Ernst Yes, yes.

Leibele In a few days, the Nazis shot Moshe Oshe-rovsky—he was the first Jew killed. He was a neighbor. He was a nice man. They called him a Communist.

Serele *Wladislav,* the bully who used to beat up the Jewish kids, snitched on him and led the Nazis to his house.

Leibele Oh, Serele, we don't know that for sure—don't say that.

Serele Mother said so.

Ernst That's not important. Go on, Leibele.

Leibele Well, the Nazis formed a Jewish Committee and my father was a member. And the Committee provided Jewish houses for them and Jewish families crowded together.

Serele My aunt and uncle and their three children came to live in our house. It wasn't crowded. We all ate and played together.

Leibele And, the Committee provided the Nazis with Jewish laborers—lawyers, and storekeepers, and the big men in the Synagogue now became plain laborers for the Nazis. And my father thought things would be quiet—then on the 9th of July—

Serele Oh, my God—

Leibele On the 9th of July the Nazis lined up 71 of our people and machine-gunned them down. They called them Communists.

Serele They lined them up in the market-square. You should have heard the screaming and the crying.

Leibele A week or so later they rounded up many of the Jewish Doctors and sent them out to the small towns. They let my father stay.

Serele We were lucky.

Leibele Then they made every Jew put a Yellow Star of David on his back—to wear it always.

Ernst You children too?

Leibele (*Pulling one out of his pocket*)
All of us.

Serele (*Takes out hers*)
I use it for a handkerchief.

Leibele Things were getting worse and worse—people were disappearing. And one night, at a big meeting in our house, *Feive,* of the Committee said: "Jews—the night of the long knife is coming near. The Nazis intend to slaughter out all of us."

Serele And then mother took us upstairs and we didn't here anymore of that meeting.

Mimi Fresh-caught fish, fresh fish.

Ernst That autumn and winter were bad.

Leibele It was the last Holy Days in the Synagogue. On Rosh Hashanah and Yom

Kippur, there was nothing but crying—the men, I mean, not only the women. And the Cantor's voice was always cracking; and on Kol Nidre the old Rabbi got up before the Ark and kept repeating: *'Gedenkt Iden, Mir Hoben a Graysen Gott.'*

Serele That means, 'Remember Jews we have a great God.' I don't know—
(She weeps)

Leibele Then on Sukkos we heard that the Jews in our neighboring towns of *Slonim* and *Lechevitch* were all butchered out.

Ernst Butchered?

Serele Not with knives—with guns. And they said they made them dig their own graves first.

Leibele Stop, Serele—you don't know that for sure. Don't always repeat what somebody said.

Serele Mother said so.

Ernst Go on, Leibele, go on.

Leibele Well my father had made an arrangement with one of his patients, a priest, the Priest Stepan.

Serele He used to wear a big silver cross and a black gown, and a black silk-like yarmulke.

Leibele (*A little impatient with her*)
Oh, that's not important. My father arranged that if anything happened to him and to mother, the Priest Stepan should try to save us.

Ernst Yes—

Leibele Well it was the first day of Chanukkah and there was snow on the ground. It was in the morning about nine—

Serele Half past eight—

Leibele (*Impatiently gesturing that she stop interrupting*)
My father was cleaning his medical tools, when there was a loud honking of a horn, and a laughing and a shouting. My father and my mother ran to the door—and we did too—and there was the *Schochet, Yosselevitch,* in front of a truck—

Serele He had a long grey beard.

Leibele (*To Serele*)
Stop—Yosselevitch fell flat on the ground with blood all over the snow. My father and my mother ran out into the street to

help Yosselevitch. Out of the truck jumped a Nazi and with a pistol shot down my father and my mother—

Mimi Fresh fish, fresh-caught fish.

Ernst Oh—
(*He embraces Leibele and Serele and they embrace him*)
No more, Leibele—don't tell any more.

Leibele No, let me tell—I want to tell—I must tell. The more we tell the better it will be for us.

Serele And then the truck ran over all three bodies back and forth—back and forth.

Leibele I quickly shut the door—bolted it, and Serele and I hid in the back above the stove and we wept quietly, and then the Priest Stepan came.

Serele He took us to his house in his church. He was so good like a grandfather.

Leibele And he kept us there for days and days.

Serele And we got different clothes and he made each of us wear a small cross.

Leibele So we should look like Christian children. But, he always asked us to pray like we

always prayed—out of this—
(*He pulls out a lovely leather-bound small book*)
out of this *Siddur* my father gave me for my Bar Mitzvah.
(*He quickly puts it back inside his blouse*)

Serele And then he took us on a train—

Leibele Yes to *Brest-Litovsk*—to a nunnery. We stayed with the nuns almost three months.

Serele They were nice.

Leibele Nazis would come in from time to time and the Mother Superior always pointed to us and said—'Such a pity, Polish orphans—one will be a nun, the other a priest.' But we were always afraid when they came.

Serele The nuns taught us Polish songs, and Catholic songs, and even Hebrew songs like they sing in the land of Israel today.

Leibele And they would teach us Polish language and French language, and we studied Hebrew by ourselves.

Serele Until Chayim came—

Ernst Who?

Leibele Chayim, Chayim Kadmi. He came one day and looked like a young priest.

Serele Very handsome—all in black.

Leibele And we learned that he was from the Hagganah underground. He came back again and again, finally he took us on a train. It was a long ride—first to Warsaw—

Serele We got off to change trains—and the station was filled with Nazi soldiers. You couldn't see a Jew.

Leibele And then another long, long ride to Budapest—with, you know, the train stopping very often and Nazis checking everybody. We never were sure—always afraid. But Chayim, in his Priest's habit kept saying: '*Sheket—hakol b'seder.*'

Serele That means—quiet, everything is in order.

Ernst (*Smiling*)
Yes, I know.

Leibele And from Budapest we managed to get to Trieste—where we stayed at an Italian Children's Camp, also under nuns.

Serele And we learned some Italian songs.

Leibele We were there till two weeks ago, when Chayim came back, this time in a Nazi uniform and took us by train to Milan and then here to Mimi's house in Marseille.

Serele Mimi's been wonderful, but we eat nothing but fish.

Mimi I love you very much, Serele.
(*She kisses her*)

Ernst (*Smiling at Mimi*)
And I always thought she was so harsh and mean.

Leibele No, no, Mimi has been like a mother to us, strict about keeping clean and brushing our teeth, teaching—and telling us to wait patiently, our ship is coming—
(*There is a bustle off stage—the Gendarme's voice is heard saying* "Bitte" *and a gruff voice answering* "Grosser Franzozischer Pferd." *The Gendarme and a young man in Nazi uniform appear—the children recognize the man immediately —they spontaneously reach out for him, Mimi and Ernst hold them back—they realize*)

Gendarme (*To Ernst*)
I'm sorry, my Captain. I told the Officer, no entrance, here—he pushed his way in,

he was reaching for his gun. I couldn't help it—

Ernst You fool—this is a German Officer. Nothing is closed to a German officer. Don't you know that?

Gendarme But you ordered no one—absolutely no one.

Ernst No one does not include a German officer. Now back to your guard and let no one come through this street. Do you hear—no one.

Mimi (*louder than ever*)
Fresh fish, fresh-caught fish.
(*The Gendarme, in utter confusion leaves stage rear. The children dash into Chayim's arms*)

Chayim Oh, Serele, Leibele—you look wonderful.

Serele Mimi was wonderful to us.

Mimi (*loud and happy*)
Fresh fish, fresh-caught fish.

Ernst (*After the children release Chayim*)
Chayim—

Chayim Ernst—
(*They shake hands and embrace*)

Mimi *(To Chayim)*
Frische fisch, bitte, Herr Capitan.

Chayim *Merci, Madame—Merci beaucoups.*
(He goes over to Mimi, pecks her on the cheek)
Mimi—you look more beautiful and smell worse than ever.

Mimi *(Laughingly, loudly)*
Fresh fish, fresh-caught fish.

Ernst Chayim—the ship's in order.

Chayim In pretty good order—she's no luxury liner, you know.

Ernst She'll get to Haifa.

Chayim Oh yes, with the children and with the guns.

Ernst *(hands him a portfolio)*
The paper, port, fleet—all in order.

Chayim *B'Seder.*

Ernst *B'Seder.*

Chayim Leibele, Serele, get your things we're going on to the ship. This is the last trip —right to the land of Israel.

Leibele We have everything—all we need—
(*He shows his prayer-book and his yellow Star of David—Serele imitating him waves her yellow Star of David*)

Chayim Good, you will join 56 children on that ship. Many are sick—long starvation—long exposure. I'm depending on you to help them—help take their fears away.

Serele We will, I know how.
(*She winks at Chayim*)
Sheket, hakol b'Seder

Leibele We will, we will—let us go.

Chayim Anything else Mimi—

Mimi Yes—take some fresh fish, some fresh caught fish.
(*She wraps several fish in a newspaper—he takes them. She embraces Serele and Leibele*)

Chayim This makes 109 children you helped us get through Ernst.

Ernst It's only the beginning, Chayim—

Chayim Good—anything else, Ernst—

Ernst Maybe—one more little thing—if they would Chayim—

Chayim Oh yes—Leibele, Serele—for our friend Ernst—would you sing, if you really feel you want to—*Hatikvah.*

Leibele Will we? We sure will.
(*The two children each grab one of Ernst's arms and sing out*)
Kol od Balevav—P'ni-Mah
Nefesh Yehudi Ho-mi-yah
(*Ernst and Chayim join in singing the words, while Mimi hums the melody*)
Ul'fa-a-se Mizrach Ka-di-mah
Ayin L'tsi-Yon Tso-fi-yah
Od Lo Avdah Tik-va-tenu
A Ha-Tikvah Ha-no-sha-a-na
La-shuv L'eretz Avo-Te-nu
L'ir ba David, David Chana—Lashuv—
(*Mimi burst out here in soprano voice with the opening words of the Marseillaise as the scene is blacked out. The light now slowly appears over stage right—the tent in the desert bringing back Ernst in his Legionnaire uniform talking with Rathenau. Mimi's break-off of the Marseillaise is picked up by the harmonica in the distance—the melody is played until Ernst resumes speaking*)

Ernst Yes, so has it been for months, with one group of children after another—from Poland, from Austria, Czechoslovakia, Romania, Hungary, the whole of Europe. With the help of Chayim Kadmi—well with the help of the Hagganah—I've managed somehow to get 143 children to Haifa so far.

Rathenau It's unbelievable—I did not know—none of us know, I guess.

Ernst It is better to keep it secret—but I want you to know that we couldn't do this without the sacrifice of a lot of good Christians. They risk their lives every hour of every day—nuns and priests and Protestant ministers, and just plain ordinary people—farmers and laborers, and housewives, and even some who are in the Nazi Army—I have contact with many of them.

Rathenau I realize that. Until Hitler came I lived and worked with thousands of good Christians. When a Christian is true to his faith he is indeed like the Christ of the Gospel. Oh, forgive me, Mon Adjutant Chef.

Ernst No, no, speak up. Speak freely here—we are free men. This is Free France. "*Liberte, fraternite, egalite.*"

Rathenau Thank you, Mon Adjutant Chef.

Ernst Yes, and when a Jew is true to his faith—to his history, to his destiny, to his mission, —you believe your people have a mission on this earth, don't you Rathenau?

Rathenau Well—I'm so confused. I'm so hurt. I really don't understand. Why all this. . . .

Ernst (*Rising and firmly*)
You haven't read your prophets for a long time—have you Rathenau?

Rathenau (*Sheepishly*)
No, I confess, I haven't.

Ernst You haven't ever read them in their original tongue, have you—in the Hebrew—in the Biblical Hebrew?

Rathenau No, Mon Adjutant Chef, I haven't. I never learned Hebrew as a child. Greek and Latin and French and English, and of course German. Yes, and I can still read in all of them—Homer and Horace in their original.

Ernst But not Isaiah and Jeremiah and Ezekiel—not Job?

Rathenau No sir, only in the translation, and very little in that.

Ernst So how can you begin to understand all this. Destiny and mission and repentance and affliction—Bah! The Nazis are taking away all the physical things from you, but you take away from yourself all that means anything in life. You've torn the soul of your people out of your being.

Rathenau (*Sadly*)
Yes Sir.

Ernst You're under my command now, Rathenau. You take orders from me. Here's a Hebrew grammar.
(*He throws it at him*)
Here's a Scripture in Hebrew.
(*He tosses it at him*)
Go to work—learn it—that's an order—and report back to me. I'll teach it to you—I'll try to give you back what belongs to you.

Rathenau Yes Sir.

Ernst You will bunk in the tent with Fauber, Pareti, and O'Hara—fine men—each one also a runaway from himself. No military duties for you—except the watch—you are ordered to study. Is that clear?

Rathenau Yes Sir.

Ernst Any questions?

Rathenau Well sir, just one—if I may?

Ernst Speak up, Rathenau.

Rathenau I hesitate sir, it's very delicate.

Ernst Speak up, man. Speak up—

Rathenau It's highly personal, Sir.

Ernst About yourself?

Rathenau No sir, about you.

Ernst Speak up, Rathenau, I'll answer if I can.

Rathenau About your own return, your repentance Sir, your making up for my uncle. May I ask sir, what brought it about? As we say in the Legion here—what triggered it? Was it indeed your reading of the Hebrew prophets—in their own tongue? Was that it?

Ernst Well, yes, in part.

Rathenau But that was so long ago sir, thousands of years ago—and many read them, I'm sure, and are not moved to anything so remarkable. Was it not something more recent than the ancient prophets? The rise of Nazis and what they are doing to us Jews, perhaps?

Ernst Yes, yes in part.

Rathenau You say, 'in part' Sir.

Ernst Yes, I say in part—
(*He moves out from behind his desk, he paces up and down the tent, rubs his face, musses his hair, then stops short and points his finger at Rathenau*)
Look here, Rathenau, you've been digging—you've been digging into my soul—deep into my conscience. Bah—I guess I dug into you and I deserve it.

Rathenau I apologize Sir.
(*He salutes and makes ready to leave, picking up the books*)

Ernst (*Sternly*)
Wait a minute. You've dug and you've struck the very core of me. Sit down—and listen like you've never listened before.
(*Rathenau sits down on the bed startled*)
There are only two people in all this shattered world who know this. You will be the third and the last. You hear me. Not a single other person on earth shall know.

Rathenau I pledge myself—Sir.

Ernst (*He almost shouts*)
On the morning of June 24, 1922, twenty years ago, I was one of those who killed your uncle, Walter Rathenau—a man I never knew—never saw. Then I learned whom I killed—one of the greatest statesmen in all the world. Had he lived there

might have been a sound Germany, a whole and wholesome Europe. Had he lived and succeeded in what he was doing there would have been no Nazis—no war. But I killed him and the guilt has been upon my heart like an immovable stone. I ran away—two days later, the day of his funeral, I came home. They got me there —they arrested me. After they took me away—that same day—my mother received a letter—

(*He takes out his wallet, and very gently removes an old browned piece of paper—almost in pieces*)

This is the letter, Rathenau, be careful with it—it has never left me from the day my mother gave it to me, twenty years ago, in my jail-cell. I've read it 10,000 times. It's a letter to my mother from the mother of Walter Rathenau—read it Rathenau!

(*Rathenau takes the letter, unfolds it very carefully, and tries to begin reading it*)

Stand up when you read that letter, Rathenau.

Rathenau (*Rising*)

Yes Sir—forgive me Sir.

(*He begins to read in a very soft voice which rises higher and higher*)

"To Frau Erika Teshow:

In grief unspeakable, I give you my hand, you of all women the most to be pitied. Say to your son, that in the name and

spirit of him who was murdered, I forgive, even as God may forgive, if before an earthly judge he make a full confession of his guilt, and before a heavenly judge repent. Had he known my son, one of the noblest men earth bore, he had rather have turned the weapon on himself. May these words give peace to your soul.
(*Rathenau pauses, emotionally exhausted, and concludes softly as he began*)
signed, Mathilde Rathenau."

END OF THE PLAY